Clean Air
Dirty Air

Lynne Patchett
Photographs by Jenny Matthews
Illustrations by Peter Bull Art Studio

A & C Black · London

Cover photographs

Front – Sticky squares test (see p. 8).
Back – Scientist testing samples of air for asbestos
pollution (see p. 10).
Title page photograph
Sticky squares test (see p. 8).

Acknowledgements

Edited by Barbara Taylor
Photographs by Jenny Matthews except for:
p.4 (bottom) Science Photo Library; p.7 (top & centre)
Morgan, p.15 Morgan, p.17 Hawkes, p.18 Morgan, p.23
Morgan, p.28 Nicholls, p.28/29 (centre) Platt, Ecoscene.

The author and publisher would like to thank the
following people for their invaluable help and
advice during the preparation of this book:
The staff and pupils of Dog Kennel Hill School and
Creswick School; Lambeth Analytical Service;
National Society for Clean Air.

A CIP catalogue record for this book is available
from the British Library.

ISBN 0–7136–3325–5

First published 1990 by A & C Black (Publishers) Ltd
35 Bedford Row, London WC1R 4JH

© 1990 A & C Black (Publishers) Limited

Reprinted 1991

Typeset by August Filmsetting, Haydock, St Helens
Printed in Italy by Amadeus

Contents

Breathing clean air   4
Why living things need clean air to stay alive and healthy,
how much air we have in our lungs

Detecting air pollution   6
Testing the air to see how polluted it is, how air pollution
affects plants, scientists at work

Smoking   11
What's in a cigarette?, smoking and health

Traffic pollution   12
Traffic fumes, why they are dangerous, lead-free petrol,
catalytic converters, electric vehicles

Winds and weather   15
How winds spread air pollution, why smog forms
over cities

The ozone layer   16
Where it is, how it protects the earth, what is causing the
damage to the ozone layer

Acid rain   18
How acid rain forms, how it affects buildings, plants and
soil, tests for acid rain, reducing the amount of acid rain

The greenhouse effect   25
What causes it, why it is making the earth warm up, how
warmer temperatures will affect the earth, how to stop the
greenhouse effect getting worse

Alternative energy   30
Making energy without making the air polluted – energy
from the sun's heat, the wind, running water or hot rocks

Useful addresses   32

Index   32

Breathing clean air

You need to breathe to stay alive. But how clean is the air you breathe? If you breathe dirty air, you are more likely to develop health problems and become ill. Plants and other animals need clean air too. Many of the things that make our lives more comfortable, such as cars and central heating, make the air dirty. Dirty air is called polluted air.

Fortunately, your body can get rid of some of the bigger pieces of dirt you breathe in. Tiny hairs in your nose and lungs trap some of the dirt. When you sneeze or cough, the dirt is thrown out of your body.

▲ In heavy traffic, cyclists sometimes wear face masks so they breathe in less dirt and fumes.

▼ This is what the walls of the tubes in a human lung look like under a powerful microscope. Can you see the clumps of hairs? In between the hairs are smooth, round cells that produce sticky mucus to trap dirt. The hairs wave to and fro to push the trapped dirt up to the throat so it can be swallowed or coughed up.

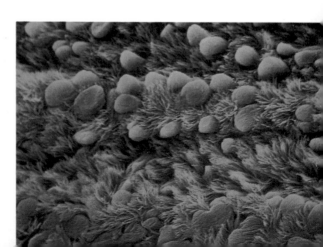

Why is breathing so important? Take a few deep breaths. Can you feel your rib cage moving in and out? This opens up your lungs so that air is sucked in. In the lungs, a gas called oxygen passes from the air into your blood. The oxygen is carried in the blood all round your body. You need oxygen so that you can use the energy in the food you eat. It is the oxygen in air that helps to keep you alive.

How much air do you need?

1 Half fill a bowl with water.

2 Fill a very large plastic bottle with water.

3 Hold the bottle over the bowl. Put one hand over the top and carefully turn the bottle upside down so the neck is under the water.

4 Put one end of some plastic tubing into the neck of the bottle and ask a friend to hold the bottle steady.

5 Mark the water level.

6 Take a deep breath and put the other end of the tubing into your mouth. Breathe out for as long as you can. What is the water level now?

The difference between the two water levels tells you roughly how much air is in your lungs. This is called your lung capacity.

5

Detecting air pollution

Can you see smoke or smell traffic fumes near your home or school? Sometimes, it is easy to work out what is making the air polluted. But to find out more about air pollution, you need to try some of these tests.

Clean leaves, dirty leaves test

Make a collection of leaves from different places and write down where each one came from. Try and collect some leaves in parks or gardens and some in streets or near factories.

Look carefully at each leaf. Is the surface shiny or dull? Does the leaf look clean or dusty? Measure the amount of dirt on each leaf by wiping over the whole leaf with a damp piece of cotton wool. Make a chart to show the differences you find.

Lichen tests

You can tell how polluted the air is by looking for plants called lichens, which are very sensitive to air pollution. Lichens grow on tree trunks, walls, roofs and gravestones. If you cannot find any lichens, this means the air is very dirty. Flat, crusty lichens mean that the air is quite dirty. Leafy or bushy lichens mean that the air is clean.

Orange crusty lichen
– dirty air

Leafy and bushy lichens
– clean air

Take a photograph of any lichens you find and mark the spot on a map of your area. Later, you can stick the photographs on your map.

7

Sticky squares test

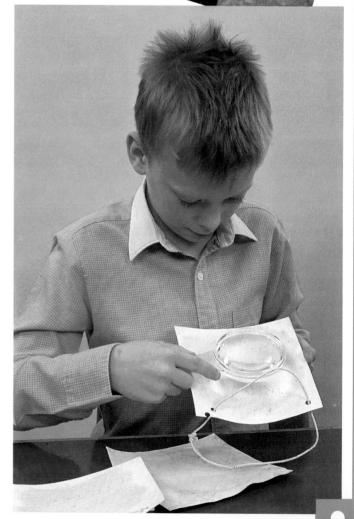

1 Cut thick cardboard or plastic into squares about 15 cm by 15 cm. Spread a thick layer of Vaseline on to one side of each square.

2 Put the squares outdoors. Choose some places where you think the air is dirty and some where you think the air is clean. Find some low places and some high places. Write the name of each place on the back of the squares.

3 After a few days, collect the squares and see how much dirt each one has collected. Look at the dirt through a magnifying glass. Which square collected the most dirt? What was the weather like while your squares were outside? How does the wind and rain affect the amount of dirt in the air?

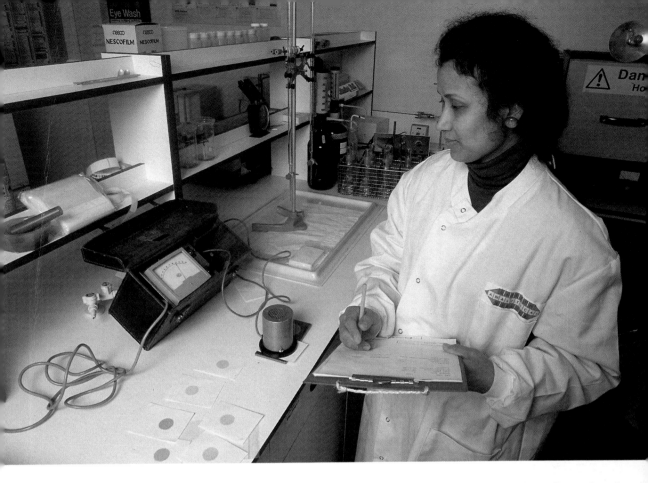

Scientists at work

These scientists are called environmental health officers. Part of their job is to test the air in their local area to find out how polluted it is. The machines they use help them to measure the amount of air pollution very accurately. Quite a lot of their work also involves answering queries about materials in the home or at work.

▲ In this test, the scientist has collected samples of polluted air from several places in a big city. She shines a light on to each sample and the needle on the machine tells her how much light is reflected. The most polluted samples reflect less light.

Bags of moss are used to collect lead, dust ▶ and other pieces of dirt from the air outside. Back in the laboratory, the moss is mixed with acid to remove the metals trapped in the moss. A small amount of the solution from the moss is placed in a machine, which tells the scientist how much lead or other metals are in the sample.

◀ Asbestos was used in buildings to stop fire spreading and to stop hot pipes cooling down. But we now know that the dust from asbestos can damage the lungs. If the asbestos in a building is crumbling to dust, it should be taken out by specially trained people wearing beathing equipment. It is important that nobody breathes in the dust from asbestos.

▼ To check that most of the asbestos dust has been removed, a sample of air is sent to an environmental health laboratory. A scientist looks carefully at the sample under a microscope and counts how many asbestos fibres are left in the air.

Smoking

Smoking cigarettes can damage a person's health. The poisons in the smoke clog up their lungs. Smokers cough a lot because their bodies are trying to get rid of all the poisons inside. Smoking may cause heart disease, lung cancer and other lung diseases. If a woman smokes while she is pregnant, her baby is more likely to be small and prone to illness.

Have you ever been in a room full of cigarette smoke? Did you cough or rub your eyes? Cigarette smoke may be harmful to non-smokers too. Breathing in air which contains other people's smoke is called passive smoking.

What's in a cigarette

* Chemicals that may cause cancer.

* Tar, which can cause lung diseases and cancer.

* Chemicals that paralyse the hairs in the air tubes so they cannot move dirt and tar out of the lungs.

* Nicotine, which is addictive, raises the blood pressure and makes the heart beat faster.

* A gas called carbon monoxide, which stops oxygen being taken into the blood.

What you can do

✷ Never start smoking.

✷ Ask people not to smoke when you are with them.

✷ Ask people who do smoke if they have tried to stop and why they think they have failed.

✷ Ask for 'no-smoking' areas in cinemas, in shops, on buses and in other public places.

Traffic pollution

Have you ever noticed that the air in a city smells different from air in the country? One of the reasons for this is all the poisonous exhaust fumes given off by the traffic in a city.

One of the gases in the fumes is carbon monoxide. Can you remember why this is harmful? Other gases may cause choking smogs (see page 15) or join up with water in the air to make acid rain (see pages 18–24). Some exhaust gases may add to the greenhouse effect (see pages 25–29).

Another dangerous substance in the fumes is the lead that is sometimes mixed with petrol to make cars run more smoothly. Lead may cause damage to the brain. Young children are especially at risk from lead poisoning.

▲ Lead can be taken out of petrol. If people use lead-free petrol, there will be less lead in the exhaust fumes and less lead to pollute the air.

There are two main ways of reducing the amount of poisonous gases given off in exhaust fumes. One way is to fit a small steel box called a catalytic converter, or CAT, into the exhaust system. Inside the CAT, chemical reactions change the harmful gases into much less harmful ones. A CAT will work only with unleaded petrol. It reduces the harmful gases by up to 90%.

Cut-away view inside a catalytic converter

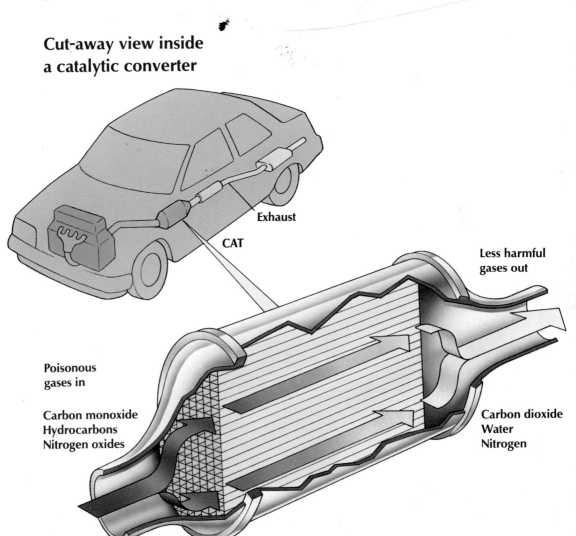

Exhaust

CAT

Less harmful gases out

Poisonous gases in

Carbon monoxide
Hydrocarbons
Nitrogen oxides

Carbon dioxide
Water
Nitrogen

The other way of reducing harmful exhaust gases is to use a different type of engine called a lean-burn engine. These engines use less petrol than an ordinary engine. When a car or other vehicle is 'cruising' at a steady speed, lean-burn engines work well. Unfortunately, whenever the vehicle goes faster, the engine gives off more harmful gases than an engine with a catalytic converter.

Electric vehicles do not give out harmful exhaust gases and they make less noise than vehicles run on petrol. But electricity is made in power stations, which pollute the air.

Instead of petrol, scientists have tried to develop vehicles that run on other fuels, such as electricity or alcohol made from plants.

Some electric vehicles are being used but their batteries may need recharging after only a short journey. Many vehicles in Brazil run on alcohol made from sugar cane. This keeps the air cleaner but the sugar cane fields take up land that could be used for food crops, villages, forests or wildlife.

What you can do

* Cycle, walk or use buses or trains rather than travelling by car. What could be done to make it easier to use bicycles, buses or trains?

* If you know someone who drives into work, persuade them to give their friends or colleagues a lift. In some cities, people who have passengers in the car are allowed to drive along a special road so they do not have to wait in traffic jams. Do you think this is a good idea?

* If the car you are in is stuck in a traffic jam for a long time, ask the driver to switch off the engine.

Winds and weather

The air around the earth is constantly moving from one place to another. Moving air is called the wind.
A strong wind can spread air pollution over a wide area.

Have you ever seen a hot-air balloon taking off? The balloon is filled with hot air, which is lighter than the cool air around it. The hot air rises and lifts the balloon off the ground. Winds are often caused by hot air rising and cool air moving in to fill the space. Air is usually warmer near the ground and cooler higher up.

Sometimes, the air near the ground cools quickly. The air higher up is warmer and traps the cool air so it can't escape. This often happens over cities in valleys. Pollution from the city is trapped near the ground and may form a poisonous mist called smog.

▼ This layer of smog trapped over Phoenix, Arizona was caused by all the fumes from car exhausts reacting with sunlight. In other places, smog may form when harmful gases from cars, factories and power stations mix with water droplets in the air.

The ozone layer

The earth is wrapped in a blanket of air called the atmosphere, which is made up of several layers. About 15–50 kilometres above the earth is a layer of gas called ozone, which is a form of oxygen.

The ozone layer is very important because it stops too many of the sun's ultra-violet rays getting through to the surface of the earth. These are the rays that cause us to tan. Too much ultra-violet can cause skin cancer. All plants and animals are harmed by too many ultra-violet rays. Life on earth could not exist without the protective shield of the ozone layer.

Every spring, a hole as big as the U.S.A. develops in the ozone layer over Antarctica. A smaller hole develops each year over the Arctic. And there are signs of a reduction in the amount of ozone all over the planet.

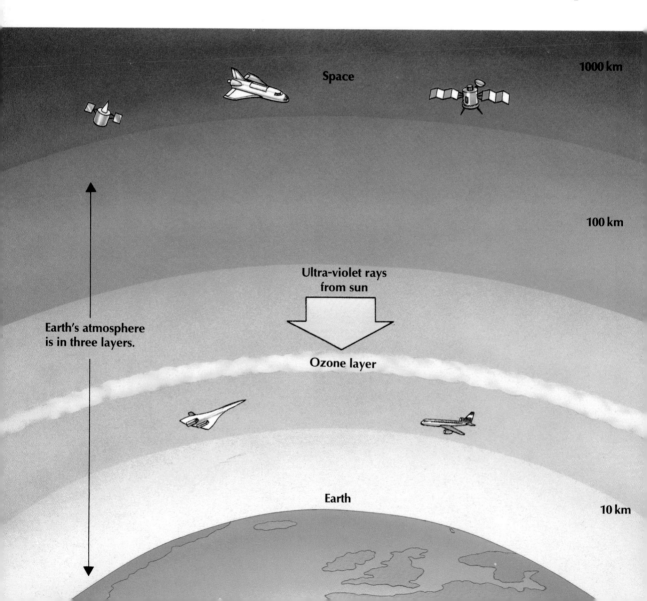

Space

1000 km

100 km

Ultra-violet rays from sun

Earth's atmosphere is in three layers.

Ozone layer

Earth

10 km

One group of gases is particularly likely to damage the ozone layer. These gases are called CFCs, which stands for **Ch**loro–**F**luoro–**C**arbons.

CFCs are used in some spray cans to force the contents out of the can. They are also used in refrigerators, air conditioning systems, some fire extinguishers and to blow the bubbles in some kinds of polystyrene. They are used because they are not poisonous and do not catch fire.

Some countries have set limits on the amount of CFCs that can be released into the atmosphere, but many scientists believe we must stop using them altogether. Tests are being carried out to find alternatives to CFCs. Do you think all companies should be forced by law to stop using CFCs in their products?

What you can do

* Buy products that don't contain harmful CFCs and try and persuade your friends and relatives to do the same. Remember that small actions by individuals can lead to big changes.

▼ Before old refrigerators are thrown away, the CFCs can be removed and used again in new refrigerators. This recycling process stops more CFCs being released into the atmosphere.

Acid rain

The stone faces on this cathedral have been damaged by acid rain. Building materials usually take many centuries to decay but acid rain makes the stone turn to dust in just a few years.

Acid rain occurs when harmful gases from power stations and vehicle exhausts join up with water in the air. Acid rain damages or kills life in lakes, rivers and forests and may help to cause some human diseases.

Strong acids work into things and 'eat away' at them. In the same way, acid rain eats away at the stones on buildings and statues and makes them crumble away.

Acid tests

To find out if a liquid is an acid, you can use indicator papers. Acids turn indicator papers red or orange. The chemical opposite of an acid is called an alkali. Alkalis turn indicator papers blue or green. See how many acids and alkalis you can find.

1 Pour a small amount of tap water, distilled water, rain-water, vinegar, lemon juice, milk and bicarbonate of soda into separate dishes. You will need to dissolve the bicarbonate of soda in water first.

2 Dip a piece of indicator paper into each dish. What colour does the paper turn? Which substance is the most acid? How acid is the rain-water? You could record your results on a chart.

Plants and acid rain test

1 Crush a Campden tablet. (You can buy these in chemists or in shops that sell things for making wine at home.) Put the crushed tablet into a glass jar and add two teaspoons of lemon juice. The mixture gives off a gas called sulphur dioxide. The gas is poisonous – stand well back and don't breathe it in. Power stations give off a lot of sulphur dioxide.

2 Put the jar into a plastic bag with some cress. Seal the bag carefully and label it. The sulphur dioxide gas from the jar will join up with moisture in the bag to make acid rain. Put some more cress into another plastic bag on its own. Seal and label this bag too.

3 After one or two days, look at the cress in both bags and record any changes that have taken place. Which of these pots of cress do you think was in the bag with the acid rain?

Acid rain damages plant growth. Conifer trees, such as pine trees, lose many of their needles. Trees that grow new leaves each year, such as oak trees, grow less leaves in summer and their leaves fall earlier than normal in autumn. Acid rain weakens trees so they are more likely to be blown over by strong winds or killed by diseases.

▲ This scientist is testing samples of air to find out how much sulphur dioxide they contain. The air is collected in bottles like the ones in the front of the picture. Inside the bottles, a chemical mixes with any sulphur dioxide in the air to make an acid liquid. The test measures how acidic each sample is.

21

Soils and acid rain test

1 Collect equal amounts of different types of soil, such as chalky soil or clay soil. Mix a little water and vinegar to make acid rain. Test with indicator paper to make sure the water is acidic. The indicator paper should turn red or orange. Put a filter paper inside a funnel and stand the funnel in a jug or beaker. Spoon one type of soil into the funnel.

2 Pour some of your acid rain over the soil and wait for it to drip through into the jug or beaker.

3 Test the water that has dripped through with indicator paper. Repeat the experiment with the other types of soil. Some types of soil react with acid rain and make the acid weaker. Chalk or limestone soils are good at this because they contain alkaline chemicals, which are the opposite of acids (see page 19). Acid soils make the problem of acid rain worse.

What can be done to solve the problems caused by acid rain?
Lime can be added to soils, rivers and lakes to make them less
acidic. The lime has to be added in large quantities and the
process has to be repeated about every three years, which is
expensive. But afterwards, plants and animals are able to live in
the water and soil again.

The main way to solve the problem is to cut down on the fumes
given off by power stations and car exhausts. In power stations,
it is now possible to remove most of the sulphur dioxide before it
is released from the chimneys into the air. This involves spraying
limestone on to the fumes inside the chimneys. Do you think
people should pay more for electricity so there is less acid rain?

23

How acid rain forms

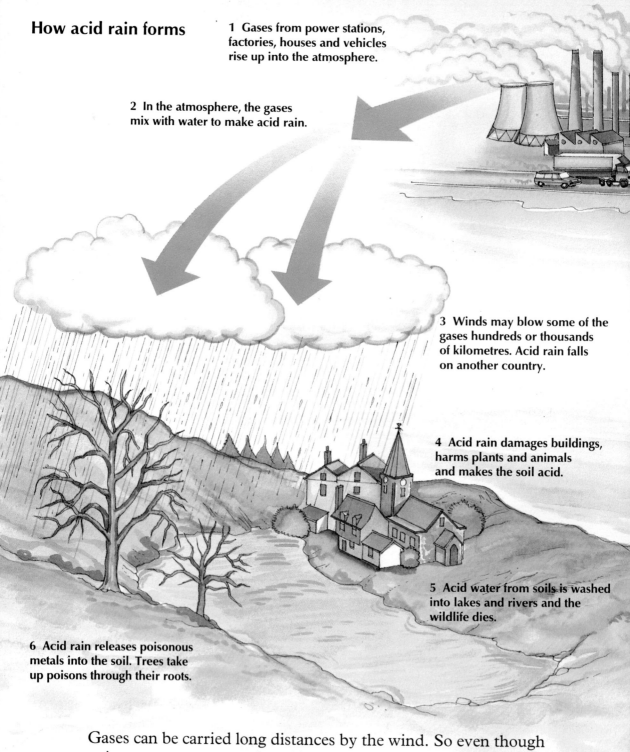

1 Gases from power stations, factories, houses and vehicles rise up into the atmosphere.

2 In the atmosphere, the gases mix with water to make acid rain.

3 Winds may blow some of the gases hundreds or thousands of kilometres. Acid rain falls on another country.

4 Acid rain damages buildings, harms plants and animals and makes the soil acid.

5 Acid water from soils is washed into lakes and rivers and the wildlife dies.

6 Acid rain releases poisonous metals into the soil. Trees take up poisons through their roots.

Gases can be carried long distances by the wind. So even though poisonous gases are produced in one country, the acid rain may fall in another country a long way away. Environmental problems often involve several countries and this makes them harder to solve. Each country has different laws and different ways of controlling pollution.

The greenhouse effect

Do you have a greenhouse at home or at school? It's hot and humid inside isn't it? The glass walls and roof of the greenhouse trap the sun's heat so the air inside is hotter than the air outside.

Many scientists think that some of the gases we dump into the atmosphere are working rather like the glass in a greenhouse. They could be trapping the sun's heat and making our whole planet heat up. This is called the greenhouse effect.

Some heat from the earth escapes back into space.

Certain gases build up in the atmosphere. These gases make it harder for the heat from the earth to push through the atmosphere out into space. So the earth becomes warmer.

Heat from the sun warms the earth.

Scientists think that if we continue to pump certain gases into the atmosphere at the same rate as we are doing now, average temperatures will rise by 2–4 degrees centigrade by the year 2030. This may not sound like much but it could cause disasters all over the world.

Some of the ice at the North and South Poles could melt, causing sea levels to rise and flood coastal areas. Three-quarters of the world's population lives on or near the coast. Changes to weather patterns could cause serious problems for agriculture and wildlife. How old will you be in 2030? Do you think you will have children of your own by then?   25

What are the gases that cause the greenhouse effect? The main greenhouse gas is called carbon dioxide. It is made up of carbon and oxygen. Green plants find carbon dioxide very useful. They use it to make their own food in a process called photosynthesis. Trees and other plants 'soak up' carbon dioxide.

How green plants make food

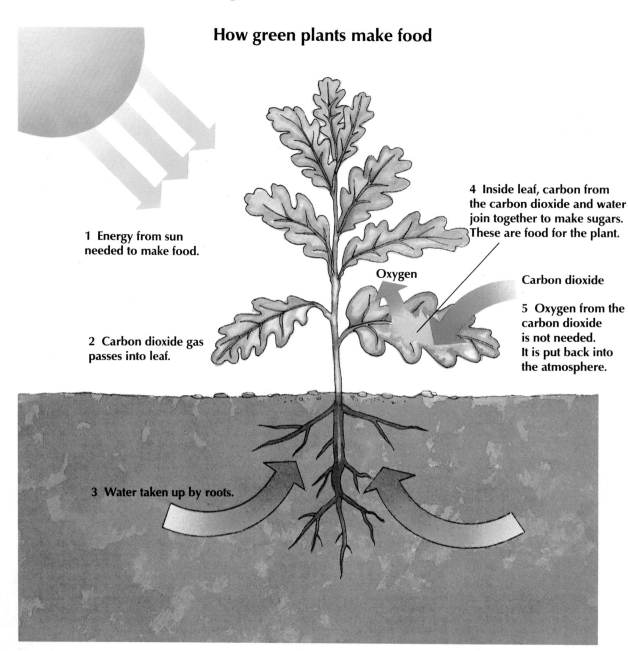

1 **Energy from sun needed to make food.**

2 **Carbon dioxide gas passes into leaf.**

3 **Water taken up by roots.**

Oxygen

4 **Inside leaf, carbon from the carbon dioxide and water join together to make sugars. These are food for the plant.**

Carbon dioxide

5 **Oxygen from the carbon dioxide is not needed. It is put back into the atmosphere.**

When animals eat plants, they take in carbon in the sugars the plant has made. So the bodies of all plants and animals contain a lot of carbon.

The carbon in plants and animals goes back into the atmosphere in two main ways. One way is when plants and animals breathe. They breathe in oxygen (see p. 5) and breathe out carbon dioxide.

The other way is when plants and animals die. Their bodies decay and the carbon is released back into the atmosphere. The path that carbon takes from the atmosphere, into the bodies of plants and animals and back to the atmosphere again is called the carbon cycle. If the delicate balance of the carbon cycle is upset, it can change the climate of the earth.

The carbon cycle

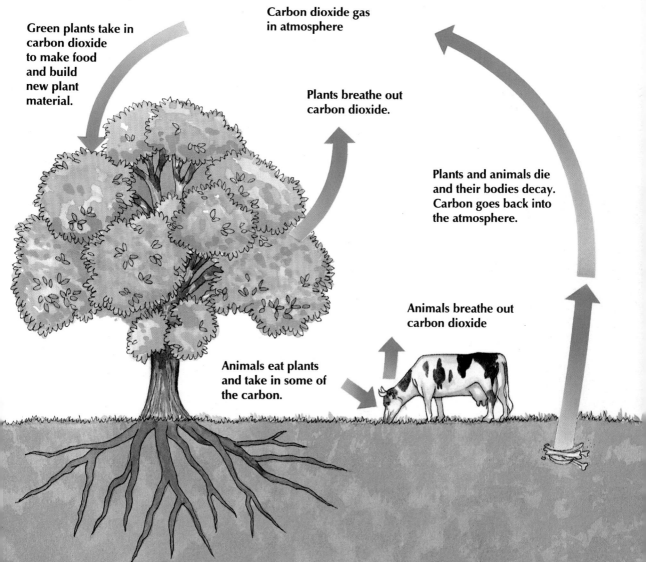

Carbon dioxide gas in atmosphere

Green plants take in carbon dioxide to make food and build new plant material.

Plants breathe out carbon dioxide.

Plants and animals die and their bodies decay. Carbon goes back into the atmosphere.

Animals breathe out carbon dioxide

Animals eat plants and take in some of the carbon.

In many parts of the world, trees are being cut down and burned at a very rapid rate. Because trees contain a lot of carbon, this increases the amount of carbon dioxide in the atmosphere and adds to the greenhouse effect. Without the trees, there are less living things to use up carbon dioxide and this makes the greenhouse effect even worse.

Many power stations burn coal or oil, which ▶ are formed from the fossilized remains of plants and animals. This puts a lot of extra carbon dioxide into the atmosphere and adds to the greenhouse effect.

▼ These trees have been cut down and burned to make way for a road through a rainforest in Australia.

Apart from carbon dioxide, some other gases are thought to add to the greenhouse effect. These include some of the gases from car exhausts, CFCs and methane. Can you remember some of the products that give off CFCs? Methane is produced in the stomachs of cattle, sheep and goats. It is also given off when waste is burned or buried. Other sources of methane are coal mines and rice fields.

What you can do

✽ Use less electricity and gas. For instance, switch off the lights when a room is not being used and wear an extra sweater instead of turning up the heating.

✽ Find out if your home is insulated. Insulation cuts down the amount of heat that escapes through the roof and walls so you will need less fuel.

✽ Eat less meat. This means there will be less farm animals producing methane.

✽ Help to plant trees, which will use up carbon dioxide.

Alternative energy

It is possible to produce energy from clean, safe sources such as the sun, the wind, water or the hot rocks deep underground. These are types of alternative energy. They do not produce gases that make the greenhouse effect worse. Unlike fuels such as coal, alternative energy has one other big advantage. It is unlikely to run out. We need to develop these methods of producing alternative energy so they are cheaper and more efficient.

◀ These solar panels on a roof of a building in Jerusalem use the sun's heat to produce electricity. Many buildings also have more glass to trap more of the sun's heat inside the building.

The hot rocks ▶ under the ground near this volcano in Nicaragua are used as a source of energy. This is called geothermal energy. It can be used to heat water or to generate electrical power. France, Iceland, Hungary, Japan, New Zealand and Britain all use some geothermal energy.

◀ Windmills can be used to lift water from wells or make electricity. They use a lot of land and have to be built in places where there is always a strong wind blowing. California has many large wind farms. For countries with not much spare land, some people have suggested building wind power stations at sea – like oil rigs. Do you think this is a good idea?

Some people think that nuclear power is the best way of reducing the greenhouse effect. It does not pump carbon dioxide and sulphur dioxide into the atmosphere. But nuclear power stations are costly to build and can cause health problems. If there are any accidents or explosions, they are very dangerous indeed. And it is difficult to dispose of radioactive waste.

Can you design and make your own model windmill? You will need to ask an adult to help you with the cutting. You will need some balsa wood, a modelling knife, thick card or plastic for the sails, some cog wheels and some elastic bands. It is a good idea to think carefully about your design before you start. Drawings will help you to work through your ideas.

Useful Addresses

If you would like to find out more about the ideas in this book, write to any of these organisations:

Action on Smoking and Health (ASH), 5–11 Mortimer Street, London W1N 7RN.
British Lichen Society, c/o Department of Botany, The Natural History Museum, London, SW7 5BD.
Campaign for Lead Free Air (CLEAR), 3 Endsleigh Street, London, WC1H ODD.
Centre for Alternative Technology, Llwyngwern Quarry, Machynlleth, Powys, Mid-Wales, SY20 9AZ.
Council for Environmental Education, School of Education, University of Reading, London Road, Reading, RG1 5AQ.
Friends of the Earth (UK), 26–28 Underwood Street, London N1 7JQ.

Friends of the Earth (Australia), Chain Reaction Co-operative, P. O. Box 530E, Melbourne, Victoria 3001.
Friends of the Earth (New Zealand), P. O. Box 39–065, Auckland West.
Greenpeace (UK), 30–31 Islington Green, London N1 8XE.
Greenpeace (Australia), Studio 14, 37 Nicholson Street, Balmain, New South Wales 2041.
Greenpeace (New Zealand), Private Bag, Wellesley Street, Auckland.
Health Education Authority, Hamilton House, Mabledon Place, London, WC1H 9TX.
National Society for Clean Air, 136 North Street, Brighton, BN1 1RG.
Watch, 22 The Green, Nettleham, Lincoln, LN2 2NR.
World-Wide Fund for Nature (WWF), Panda House, Weyside Park, Godalming, Surrey, GU7 1XR.

Index

acid rain   12, 18, 20, 21, 22, 23, 24
animals   4, 23, 24, 26, 27, 29
asbestos   10
atmosphere   16, 17, 23, 24, 25, 26, 27, 28, 29, 31
Australia   28

batteries   14
Brazil   14
breathing   4, 5, 10, 27
buildings   18, 24

California   31
carbon cycle   27
carbon dioxide   26, 27, 28, 29, 31
carbon monoxide   11, 12
cars   4, 12, 13, 14, 15, 18, 23, 24, 29
catalytic converter   13
CFCs   17, 29
cigarettes   11
coal   29, 30
cycling   4, 14

electricity   14, 23, 29, 30, 31
electric vehicles   14
energy   5, 30, 31

environmental health officers   9, 10

factories   6, 15, 24
food   5, 14, 26, 27

geothermal energy   30
greenhouse effect   12, 25, 26, 27, 28, 29, 30, 31

health   4, 11, 16, 18, 31
human body   4, 5, 10, 11

insulation   29

lead   9, 12
lean-burn engine   13
leaves   6, 21, 26
lichens   7
lungs   4, 5, 10, 11

metals   9, 24
methane gas   29

nicotine   11
nuclear power   31

oxygen   5, 11, 16, 26, 27
ozone layer   16, 17

passive smoking   11
petrol   12, 14

photosynthesis   26
plants   4, 20, 21, 23, 24, 26, 27, 28, 29
power stations   14, 15, 18, 20, 23, 24, 29, 31

rainforest   28
recycling   17
refrigerators   17
rivers   18, 23, 24

smog   12, 15
smoking   11
soil   22, 23, 24
sulphur dioxide   20, 21, 23, 31
sun   15, 16, 25, 26, 30

temperature of the earth   25
traffic fumes   4, 6, 12, 13, 14, 15, 18, 23, 24, 29
trees   7, 21, 24, 28, 29

ultra-violet rays   16
unleaded petrol   12, 13

waste   29
weather   8, 15, 24, 25
wildlife   14, 24, 25
windmills   31
winds   8, 15, 21, 24, 30, 31